A City Grows

Susan Ring

This is Chicago. It is one of our country's biggest cities. Millions of people live and work in Chicago.

Let's find out how Chicago began, and how it grew. This is how the same place looked many years ago.

Native Americans were here first. They settled on the land near this river, which they named "Checagou."

Fort Dearborn

In 1803, Fort Dearborn was built along the river. Chicago started as a group of buildings around this fort.

This picture of Chicago was drawn in 1833. Four years later, Chicago was big enough to be called a city.

CHICAGO IN 1833

By the 1850s, Chicago had become a big city.
It would soon become one of the largest
lumber centers in the world.

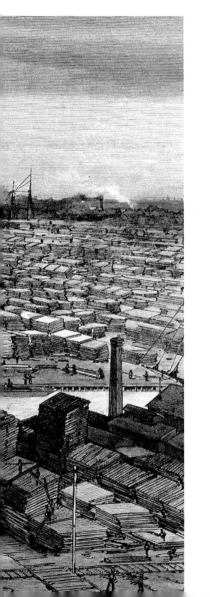

Ten years later, the city had grown so much that, by the 1860s, it had fifteen railroad lines. Now it was easy for people to get to Chicago by water and land.

Many ranchers brought their cattle to Chicago stockyards to sell.

By 1870, the city was growing rapidly and people needed homes built quickly. Chicago had a lot of lumber, so homes were made of wood.

Sidewalks were made of wood, too. Even some of the streets had wood in them. The people did not know what was going to happen to their city because of all that wood.

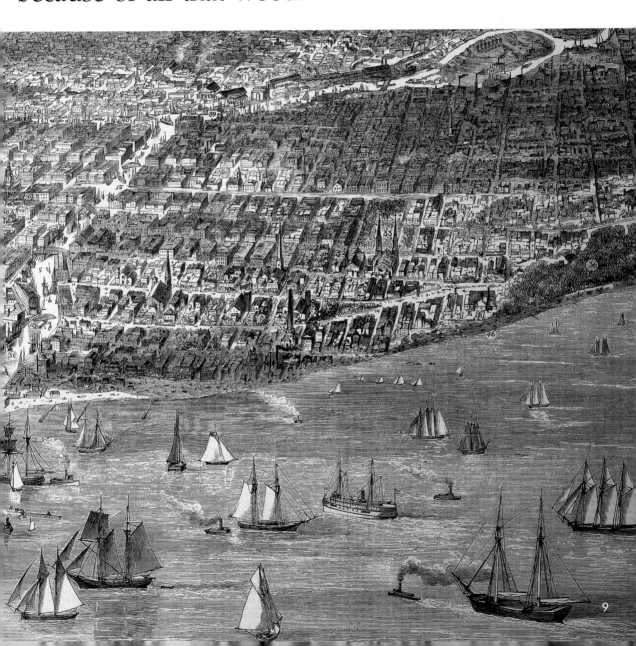

On the night of October 8, 1871, a huge fire started in Chicago. No one knows for sure how it began. Some people have said it started when a cow kicked over a lit gasoline lantern.

The fire spread quickly and burned for hours. All of the wooden houses, sidewalks, and even the streets were in flames. The city was almost totally destroyed.

But the people of Chicago worked hard to rebuild their city. In only one year, hundreds of new homes, factories, and stores were built.

Chicago was growing into a bigger city than before the fire. In 1885, the world's first skyscraper was built there. It was just nine stories high!

Today, Chicago is home to the tallest building in the United States. It is called the Sears Tower. This skyscraper is 110 stories high.

Chicago is also home to one of the busiest airports in the United States. Chicago has grown to be one of the most important cities in the world.

Chicago Time Line

1833 · THE CITY GROWS

By 1833, the city of Chicago begins to grow as people build houses and other buildings around Fort Dearborn.

1850s · LUMBER CENTER

By the 1850s, Chicago was becoming one of the largest lumber centers in the world. Logs were sent to factories in Chicago to be made into boards.

1871 · FIRE!

In 1871, there was a huge fire in Chicago. It burned for hours, destroying much of the city.

1885 · THE FIRST SKYSCRAPER

The world's first skyscraper was built in Chicago in 1885. It was only nine stories high.

TODAY · SEARS TOWER

Today, you can find the tallest building in the United States in Chicago. It is called the Sears Tower, and it is 110 stories high.